walking in snow

by

john knoepfle

indian paintbrush poets

Copyright © 2008 by John Knoepfle. All rights reserved.

Published by Indian Paintbrush Poets, an imprint of Pearn and Associates, Inc., Boulder, Colorado.
For information about our products and services please contact us at happypoet@hotmail.com, (720) 406-8858.

Cover design by Anne Kilgore.

Acknowledgements

Thanks to the editors of the following newspapers, literary magazines and books, which previously printed some of the poems in this collection: *Illinois Times, National Catholic Reporter, The MacGuffin, New Letters, The Other Side, I Look Around for my Life,* Pearn and Associates, Inc., and *The One Instant and Forever,* Illinois Wesleyan University.

I wish especially to acknowledge the late Martina Kocher for her translation from the German of Georg Friedrich Daumer's "Polydora," which Brahms used for the *Liebeslieder Waltzes.*

Library of Congress Control Number: 2008930055

Knoepfle, John 1923
walking in snow, by John Knoepfle. First Edition.
ISBN 978-0-9777318-7-9 paper.

for peggy, as always
especially the waltzes

contents

pictures from ireland

ancient church with tower *3*
winter morning *4*
ruins *5*
river with evergreens *6*
communal poem *7*
children sledding *8*
dawn *9*
rope yarn sunday *10*
middle of march *11*
slante *12*
who was it waited here *13*

from a residency at illinois wesleyan university

prayer room poem *17*
second prayer room poem *18*
gift of john wesley powell *19*
stage behind mcpherson hall *20*
fall night *21*
october break *22*
campus at daybreak *23*
when the residency ends *24*
meditation *25*
fall evening *26*

four cats

    sam *29*
    meepy *31*
    cat poet *32*
    old ace from otis street *33*

lines from
the liebeslieder waltzes

    now bitterness darkens my eyes *37*

before dawn poems

    first day of the month *47*
    early morning *48*
    waiting for dawn *49*
    last sunday in january *50*
    thoughts on my birthday *51*
    well yes a valentine *53*
    feast day and memorial day celebration *54*
    9/11 the aftermath *56*
    halloween *57*
    veterans day *58*
    alone and what to say *59*

old johns miscellany

tornado watch 63
weapons in space 65
words in dejection 66
vision 67
winter coming on 68
distances 69
sister miriams poem 70
bench with old men 71
blue beads 72
meditation on bach 73
grandmother 74
check up 75
poet and pond with ducks 76
noontime 77
morning of the wedding 78

northern lights

mountain above anchorage 81
surprise glacier 82
down from the mountains 83
ladies of the klondike 84
piece of cloth 85
fort richardson memorial day 86

the christmas revels

    this christmas eve *89*
    collage for the year turning *89*
    well now a christmas card *90*
    then on that starstruck night *90*
    the wise men came later *91*
    when christ came to town *92*
    our lady our mother *92*

epilogue

    lines for a new beginning *94*
    walking in snow *95*

pictures from ireland

ancient church with tower

how bright this world seems
there is a trace of gold
hidden in that polished lawn

even the unkempt graves
seem nourished on so clear a morning

and there centered a great tower
points with the hand of faith
a message written for the sky
the prophet keeping his watch

on the heights there are
the last remnants of snow
postscripts from the winter

everything seems to be
constructed from angles
except for the far sky

haven beyond understanding
gift of compassion
lost voices where are you singing

winter morning

here is a bridge
and a creek running below
frozen solid as the morning

there are houses
locked against the dawning cold
even the light seems shivering
tree limbs would snap
if a stiff wind came on

it has been a restless gathering from sleep
this slow breaking day
the mind should have been quiet
content with the drift into morning

well yes there is something to be said
for the old great winters when even the birds
kept a puffed and shivering peace
my hands are cold

ruins

it is a better morning
it is possible to say this
a pale blue sky oversees the haze
the hills are no longer softened
they are etched now

old stone walls are visible
the winds have come here
and shepherded the snows away

and I can see now
there are ruins in these hills
tangible stones left there
how long a thousand years
for solitaries on these heights
who made their prayers in common

they lived in a world that did not need lies
their world a testament to their hope

these ruins cannot be ruins
these are the visibilities of ancient chants
testimonies to hope

these stones are keepsakes
for the bones of fathers

and women those weavers of sandals
who walked into the heavens
and carried the spirit down

river with evergreens

a stream here so peaceful beyond us
hidden in a curtain of spruce
I think they must be norways

you always want to know
be able to say what a thing is

this concentration on thingness
taking the mind off of itself
the foibles the unmentionables
those hidden places of self disquiet
where the world makes no judgment
and we condemn only ourselves

the stream is for the taking
we dip our cupped hands
trailing the water
and we are able to drink

communal poem

here is a retreat
a sylvan place
flowers and green shadows

the day is cool
there are dog violets
a social of bluebells

a damp fertile place
the world recreating itself

it is time to abandon
the caution of success
time to turn the radio down
denature the tv screen

time to listen and watch
listen and watch

children sledding

their world could never be level
and this day the slopes are the best
mantled with ridges of solid snow

I will say this about them all
they are plum cheeked and shouting
and here this one has a bright red parka
and this one is running
his left foot arching behind his forward stride
and this tyke is decked in black with gold trim

and everyone is leaping in the air
it is cold and they are all blowing steam
the slope ahead the best they could remember
and they batten down on their old sleds
until exhaustion sends them home

and they trail off in twos and threes
yes home perhaps for hot cocoa
or thick suppers of potato soup
and then on to dreamless sleep

something they did not earn
and no one tells them they have to

dawn

under the great clouds
a premonition of daylight
here are the spires
the onion shaped domes
here the crosses
loft a resurrected sky

the morning sun
demonstrates the nature of fern to fern

and we begin again

rope yarn sunday

the sea and the things of the sea
this morning unfurling
how wonderful it is this day
this dawn this lighthouse this wind
all things in place
and that brave ship off the point
I have known that eagerness aloft
wind howling in the rigging
I do not need to look up

middle of march

it is that time again
we have to pick up the rocks
clear the roads again
whatever is left over from winter

would you be having a pint

slante

I have read how in uganda
the president of ireland
protected from the lepers
abandoned her speakers platform
and went down to shake hands
with every sick bodied soul
who came to hear her
until they shouted with joy

I pray the god of the heavens
hold you in his hands
and bless your compassionate fingers

who was it waited here

what celtic father
kept his watch
waiting for whoever would come
from an improbable distance

a son perhaps
unbinding his fathers eyes
healing them with a blessing
with magnificence
setting them free
with spittle and dust

not that this would be easy

the odds are not good
he knows this
gets up in the morning
remembers his evening star
dancing in time

from a residency at
illinois wesleyan university

prayer room poem

stained glass
window facing south
miraculous blues and reds
when the sun
jewels the prophets day

students come to this room
write their thoughts in spiral notebooks
argue back and forth
their affirmations their
forthright denials
an honesty of innocence
shaming my cautious age

are we yet alive

second prayer room poem

commemorated here
those who died in the torpedoing
of the uss dorchester
february 3 1943

george fox
john washington
alexander goode
charles poling

died praying together
refusing the overcrowded lifeboats
their jackets given to others

four chaplains
a minister
a minister
a rabbi
a priest

so memorable a text
all that they could be
they were

gift of john wesley powell

water jar the zuni world
polychrome white and brown
these fantastic birds
and here grazing below them
those familiar pronghorns
where the zuni have a middle world

this pot holds all creation
all the world the zuni knew
its air earth fire and yes
that dream of clear running water

and nothing disturbs this world
not even my breath this noontime
forming its own small country
on the glass display case
above that parched universe

the one world of the zuni

stage behind mcpherson hall

this space so empty in the wind
a silence this evening where it seems
only that silence itself has meaning
until one long night in a thousand
this nondescript shred of humanity
creeps into a surprise of light
an apology coming forward on that stage
a man trembling with uncertainty
that no one has ever heard of

and then he lifts up the mask
so clearly visible and yet so unseen
and adjusts it to his face
and there he stands and he is seven feet tall
and his words turn the dark night to stone
I am oedipus and I am the king of thebes
and from out of nowhere an audience
responds from a bruised heart
with revulsion and the shock of pity

fall night

blue velvet sky
stars in their dormitories

they are like students

even when they are awake
they are asleep

october break

why did she abandon this cup
tea still drying in the bottom
white cup with its green collar

preoccupied I guess
going home for fall vacation
and her mother with a lap full of worry
little brother using her barbies for spears
her father disturbing the sunday
with his new riding mower

it is autumn
and a scattering of leaves

it is amazing
how helpless she will be loving them
but that will come later

campus at daybreak

christopher wren red brick
romanesque palladian
the measured stones of this campus

it is a cold morning
my fingers are numb
the cushions of my palms aching

a freshening wind
an arching sun in a eastern sky

it will be a good day
I know it will be a good day
I will taste and savor and know

when the residency ends

it is only in the
unfolding of the rose
that you know
the pulse of the rose

and the giver

when something goes dark
behind your eyes

meditation

wind harries the leaves
across this campus

the midmorning sun
dapples the sidewalks
with the shadows of maples

and the silence of this hour
that is the invisible shadow

where the students pass me
reaching for their own lives

su shi saw the clouds
breaking into pieces
he tipped his wineglass into the river
when his vision faded

the artist
considers one stroke
and the paper reforms

fall evening

the evening so still
the trees shape the silence

campus gentled to an amber glow

voices of students
a thousand miles away

favorite stars
the wain there

jet liner some high
silent moth crossing the sky
I could hold it in my hand

but I need to move along
recreate the creation
day by day this dark hour

so much could be lost
the other side of silence

four cats

sam

well sam your white whiskers
they are a national treasure

how remarkably they express
that velvet black face you claim your own
it is a face only a senator of cats
would carry in the halls of deliberation

oh you know when to institute
progress through legislation
or when to hiss the clumsy ploys
senatorial toms foist on your republic

old buddy we have years in common
we have both expended more lives than most
and have yet to count through nine
and only this morning
you challenged your arthritic bones
and lapped from the toilet bowl
what a triumph that was for your old legs

you only pretend you need
a footstool to leap up on the bed
how well you understand
the human condition auden spoke of
how your mistress and your master
will rush to serve you
when you offer a simple meow

I will not go on
you do not need my praises

I will say only that you can double
the very image of yourself
when the kitchen overhead light
gleams to touch your shadow

meepy

meepy fine old white and gray
oh marvelous cat sitting upright
your four paws contiguous
cat for a pharaoh to bow to
or a master of zen to envy
and who would dare annoy you
calling your name
expecting that you would cuddle
a peaceful afternoon in his arms
when you meditate a world away
wandering the dark matter
roiling your catabolic universe
oh philosophical puss
it is not that you are unfriendly
it is only that like plato
you are thinking of something else
when aristotle strolls by

and yet for all that
a cats a cat at bedtime
and here you come
poking my forearm with your vertical frown
saying how to you like my ears
and falling asleep then
so calmly in dreams of a walled garden
and a cats meow in paradise

cat poet

I trust that you will notice that I
am the cat piscataway
because I am once from new jersey

you may wish to admire my coat
sleek gray with black stripes
and memorable touches of cinnamon

I am mrs mcgowans friend
and I am the resident poet
which I have been since 19 and 72
during which time I have composed
all of the professors poems

there are some who admire my baudelaire
would you like to scratch my ears

come in yes come into the house
we will call for a saucer of milk
and if you will pardon my french
you will enjoy a very nice chatte

old ace from otis street

it was in washington d c
this old gray tomcat joined us
he had a slightly closed left eye
and his ears were somewhat jagged
and maybe he walked with a limp
as he was clearly a veteran
of more than one back alley skirmish

he had no trouble at all adopting us
made himself a home in this
pad of five or more scholars
he listened with pleasure to our vivaldi
as he was veteran himself of four seasons
yes and nine lives more I would say
and el salon mexico was a favorite
and he was a paw print artist
and he had purrfect excitement
whenever someone came in with groceries
he would meow him
all the way to the kitchen

and what was his value
this companionable old tom
well pity the moth fluttering along the wall
he would flash his great old paw
and our student world
was one arrogant bug the less

lines from
the liebeslieder waltzes

now bitterness darkens my eyes
and where were you when the stars
fell out of heaven

oh my darling
when you want to call me
I know that I will hear you

this rush of wild water
racing through granite escarpments

where are you now
what would your love teach me

the river is clear and deep
beyond the falls

if it were not for your love
I could not have found
my one true vocation

I kiss your hands
they are filled with starlight

my lovely girl do not pout
a sadness that gutters today
will be trimmed for laughter tomorrow

the little bird came
and when you held out your hand
it kept an easy balance

I would be comfortable
reading your lifeline

I know that wherever I am
whatever massive stadium I visit
that I can find you

I will see you smiling
no matter how great the crowds

but do not frown
oh if you frown
all the birds will weep
and my favorite team
will lose the match

I know now
whenever you turn to me
I cannot be sad

when you smile
I carry an olympic torch
everywhere in the world

nothing will keep you from me
I will travel our great heartland river
I will hitch a passage on your towboat
I will be your first mate

when love finds love
pulses are beating in time

the world is full of glum lovers
even if they say I am a madman
I will never be one with them

evil thinking kills love
steely eyes will tell you this

what they have to say
will wither a blossoming love

it is april
the doves fluff out their feathers
male to female

there will be a new nest
hidden in the magnolia
but even an old one will do
they are not particular

the full moon can see
the very bottom of our world
shipwrecks on the coral reefs
the yardarms are polished silver

mockingbirds
they call and respond
hour after dark hour

I remember your kisses
I want to return them

sometimes the chain
falls deep down the cistern

do you know what I mean

oh lover where have you gone
this lonesome night

fireflies in the corn fields
they astonish the country roads
a lover in tears does not see this
so deep that darkness

I have known yes
that shiver in the soul
when love falls away from a lover

this can be measured in pain
but not the warm hour
when love comes home

before dawn poems

first day of the month

sleet rain in buckets
wind to knock out your teeth
showers of ice
then the snow batters the house

water in the basement
cold shaking the windows
even the christmas lights
blinking an emergency

now in the morning
you scrape the car windows
unlock the left front door
with a hair drier

and look here the sun
comes beaming out of the east
says old man why not smile
everything is forgiven

you stand there in the cold
studying your frozen fingers
wondering what the hell
was it you did that was wrong

early morning

sounds from the kitchen
a jar set on a counter perhaps
plates gathered a glass
now a freezer door closing
and now another sliding open
and forks and spoons in a jangle
a spigot turned and water

what time is it
yes early for a sunday
and now the refrigerator door
opens and shuts again

now suddenly the silence
someone reading the newspaper
yes perhaps that
it would be something political
on this political morning

I have been at sixes and sevens
disturbed of late
so these kitchen sounds a consolation
those capable hands at small tasks
hands that have known mine
that I have held in mine
all these many years

waiting for dawn

no noise this darkness at four
only the trickle of water
the little rill among the house plants

how to get this right
so solemn an hour
this priceless moment
I know I will not see it again

there are four messages
a student who outlasted the sixties
craftsman now for slate roofing
a colleague who shared rengas
an editor with a good heart
a women from the upper mississippi
who dreams of peace

they all live to redeem
the stupidities of these sad times

they are with me in this silence
they wait as I wait for a privilege
the utter peace of this hour before dawn

I turn off the computer
it is time to be still

last sunday in january

well almost to february
and then the springtide coming
but we had snow this evening
and my neighbor across the street
turned on her christmas lights

the roads were slick too this morning
on a foggy sunday
but now the sun labors west
and the streets are clear

my neighbor cheered us
giving us her small vigils
along the fence there in her front yard
so I want to thank her for that

this is a sunday for beatitudes
for lives we live and do not live
and saint brigit of killdare will follow
she of the springtime

I am just talking here
you know that and yet
something may come of it
some small illumination
something given that was not
a necesssary offering

thoughts on my birthday

I am already expendable
talk about deficit spending
where has my life gone
where is it going today tomorrow

I am looking at this picture
a fir or pine it is hard to say
there is a hotel or a hostel
the other side of a lake
just to the right of a creek
the mouth entering there

you are wondering
what is this all about
the old man is wandering
his thoughts spilling like agates
well this is the way I feel today
people want to be perfect
they don't have time for anything
and nothing is forgiven

well I don't know
am I talking about myself
or somebody else

well this is what happened today
a little girl woke up from the dead
she was one of the rare ones
and she was hungry as you can imagine
and maybe her mother went crying
over the stove fixing that little child
pancakes with butter and maple syrup

there was this woman too
I don't know how old she was
but she had been bleeding twelve years
and her husband he must have
fallen on his knees
and streaked his eyelids with dust

and the families were hugging
oh after the long waiting
an overflowing of tears
and all of them dancing in their underwear

I don't care how this is going
I am over eighty I was born this day
that was in 1923 at two in the morning
my mother never blamed me
being kept up so late
she was like the woman like the little girl
filled with laughter and those tears

well yes a valentine

I did not forget what day this is
and it is a half century now
and yes we have known
a stormy sea or two
well what else would you expect
petrachs old brig sailing on
whatever we would do to sink it

I just wanted to tell you
that I know I am not always good at this
but then who is better come to think on it

I just wanted to say something to you
something about the holy martyr
and birds in the cathedral nooks
puffing their feathers on this day

and lady that I know given this day
that you have made me one of the lucky ones

and so sweetheart here is my valentine
and are you surprised that I still have
your blue garter so faded now
oh yes that was when the bridegroom
cheered the hour laughing in his tent
because it was mine all mine

and so I want to tell you
how I love you to the quick
and nothing can change that

feast day and memorial day celebration

what should we be saying
how abject the loneliness this morning
this sunday and one day before
memorial day and celebrated now
the old thursday feast
the apostles gazing into heaven
until the angels wanted to know
why on earth were they staring there

this is a mixed up business
some sense that when this page is turned
there will not be another
and yet there will be another

well I don't know why but I guess
it all has something to do with that
purple heart hung on the framed
caleb bingham stump speaker

I will go to the cemetery tomorrow
and I have set our colors in the wind this morning
and last year there were old men with me
they were standing around
I don't know trying to think of
something they might be saying

there were several all dressed up
and full of humor for reporters
and I cannot tell you why
old hands I guess at public functions

I wonder is the pain deeper
the older you are coming to these events
or is it you carry a burden for all those
lost along the way
those you did not know
as if a slow wisdom
set a heavy price for you
a gift left from those who went ahead

well I don't know
I do know you look for light
when the darkness comes on
and I have to say old friends
whatever you leave me tomorrow
I will hold however I can

9/11 the aftermath

where were we that day
wherever home was
breathing the dead sadness of the morning
watching the smoke
from living rooms of grief
the morning held in handcuffs
I have this mask of stunned rage
it carves my face

today there is a video
these improbable americans
carrying their griefs to afghanistan
those who lost eternities
when the towers went down
gone to that high country
touching those others
who live with their own dead
victims of our errant bombings
sad lives bound to one another

and in the white house
and in the halls of congress
where are the pilgrims
the living who share the dead

halloween

how fine this morning
that big orange pumpkin
there on the western horizon
you can see the craters
or as the peoria would have it
their old woman
putting out brush fires

now when I look up
the moon is gone
but not what I remember

veterans day

and I remember there was a woman
sprawled on a path in okinawa
her face in the dirt her black dress hitched
above her knees her legs already swollen
and the little pot that death thieved from her
all her maternal caring
spilled on the path beyond her fingers

I asked the chaplain
what would become of her
he told me through cigarette smoke
a bulldozer would put her under
that was the day after easter

no ancestral tomb for her
no sealed gate on okinawa

and today a day for veterans
I did not like the songs
I heard touted on radio and television
and in the evening watched with friends
the documentary on surgeons in iraq
and their faithful assistants
and soldiers and wounded marines joking
and those purple hearts on the bared chests
and ill fated iraqis hauled in from car bombs
and that chaplain with his prayers
hoping to fit the right words for the dead

alone and what to say

sitting here in the fading dark
I study my weathered hands
a dog barking across the street
shambles the morning

it is a quarter to five

well now with this survey
there are many questions
where did we come from
where will we be going

I know the first of course
yes where I came from
but where will we be going
is a poser

maybe our dead can teach us
mail us their dissertations

it can never be easy
giving up what we do not need
theres the rub
my left hand bends with a shadow
gone to the right

old johns miscellany

tornado watch

well how many days have gone now
how many since the windy night
came with a roar from the west
snapped off tree branches thirty-five feet up
great old timers those squirrel havens
owl roosts or hawk watches
left standing with bare limbs

it is the caprice the inhumanity of luck
rips this neighbors roof off
spares the robins clutch next door
tangles and snaps the power lines
great poles left to their old dead angles

well we did survive with ancient skills
overcoats in icy living rooms
a candle flickering in the kitchen
extra coats and blankets on the beds

neighbors who never had thought about
any need to talk to one another
clearing yards of fallen trees next door
this is what is remembered
the moment we knew our neighbors

that was after the wind whirled east of us
and the darkened houses emptied
and the streets went wandering with shadows
and you could hear voices you had not heard before
"are you all right are you all right"

we have gone back to our old routines now
and strangers driving through
would not notice the snapped off trees
and we will all seem to be what we were

weapons in space

rabbi what do you say
what when the golem of prague
strides above our small world

that golem in the old days
was brought to civility
when men of consequence
diminished him

but rabbi the new power
the one launched to dirty the heavens
it struts and postures beyond our vision
what of this one
released for our dust and ashes

what of the end of the world
what of that moment
when time itself vanishes

who will mourn for us
care that we ever existed
who will say kaddish for us

rabbi teach us this day
how we may be made complete
how we can say shalom

words in dejection

after the beer it is the television
that is turned off you wonder
what place you have been given to lose
it seemed we had something planned
some gentle browsing
old lovers night out as I remember

but this has gone by the wayside
there is so much more that craves attention
after all the world needs looking after
and every hour there is something unholy
like a mouth of hunger begging satisfaction

I have this pictured to think on now
there are three oaks
and a lake back of them
the sky above driven with clouds
and of course a morning sun
replenishing the oaks until they become
antiquities of beaten gold

well all right

vision

you always want to
watch from a high place
take your time keeping watch
being careful until you know
what it is you are seeing
you are seeing

this is so simple
you need two good eyes
but even one will do and there are people yes
who are fairly good watchers
who have no good eyes at all

they can read a thousand miles
and touch a small girl
a three year old perhaps
who gleans baby food jars
from trash heaps in guatemala

they see the child
taking her careful way
among cast out wraps from hospitals
or spent needles off the streets
and they know that she
will live but a year more or two
and they would offer her
their poor eyes

others see the great world

winter coming on

rain all day this day
heavy downpours
bad day for street people
and this on all hallows

what happened yesterday
well there was a bad flight
had us sucking in our bellies
but the pilot knew his business
and we survived

perhaps like the nation
pray god we come along
better than we have earned
and this sunday the news
nine more marines
dead in iraq

how would the prophet
finish this poem
or the compassionate
witch of endor
what would she say

reader what do you say
it is deep into fall
and the heavens dark
our sun gone into hiding

distances

mist hung hills beyond hills
rising where the eye scarcely reaches them
all bathed in pale ambers subdued whites
the foreground sloping to the left

not easy to read this perhaps
this rediscovering some far off text
so quiet in the calm of the morning

there is a stone pile on the right
it is a stubbornness
a thing handsome in itself
where nothing else matters

I know the man
the one waking
who stares at the familiar
without seeing

sister miriams poem

now a dark matter
our perfumed space
polished with light
and a woman combing her hair
beyond existence
beyond our coming and going

where his sandals were
a scent lingering from compassion
the blast of crude nails
could not change this

the old sister will tell you
martha did her part
she expects you will get the point
figures you are as wise as she is

she will be wrong of course

bench with old men

after dawn brings in the daylight
there will be a bench
where several can be seated
and they will speak of everything
like old men who wander to the drugstore
maybe in auburn or st louis
go there for morning coffee together

nothing slips beyond them
they remember everything
everything that happened in their world

for those who come to this bench
let there be a valley stretched out below
a place of small towns and cities
and far opposite let there be
a range of hills and let these be sunlit

the old men are patient with their shadows
they know the sun will come to them
and it will warm them when it comes

blue beads

blue beads from the dirt floor
the slave house in central missouri
close there to arrow rock
and the river ports along the way

why are the beads important
some memento trailing from africa

and now I am told
twenty-five hundred of our troops
have died in iraq
for an official voice which says
we are fighting a war on terror

it is corpus christi
the old feast from 1264
a figure for a joyful memorial
transubstantiated a lock of white
papal hair restless in the wind
a host lifted beyond sunrise or sunset

and yesterday the world cup
and that most famous anthem
when germany bested poland
by the one single goal

good woman I have heard you
I want to give you back your blue beads
I want you to rise from the dead
I want you to live forever

meditation on bach

bach of the many children
feverish composer this morning
harpsichord concerto in d minor
fingers rushing a breathless charge

reading this article
things to know about kissing
smirking hot from cosmopolitan

I am amazed
all the authorities
knowing twenty year olds
the far side of reality

a magazine for women
I read the want ads
I guess all remarkable kissers

bach is resting
conjuring lost concertos
enlivening his youth yes

his loved woman
was black in the sunlight
a bride of solomon

the old man looks up from his composition
he is smiling

grandmother

her prayers were
so simple
so straight forward
so unselfconscious

when they were
known in heaven

god wept

hey old lady we asked her
please open the door for us
when we want to come home

she would tell us
the good thing about marriage is
you can throw pillows with impunity

and how does all this
come about we wondered

well she told us
it has something to do
with honor and time and value

yes it is a variation
conjugal that is

check up

I have this itch down the center of my back
where it is impossible to reach it
my feet feel like they are on fire sometimes
sometimes it is like walking on pins and needles
the itch also moves around from day to day
it seems to be on a petty pace
one time between the fingers
another high on my behind and so on
when I walk I often feel out of balance
I have a low grade headache usually
I wake up in the night with and contend
for several hours with various monsters
then the birds begin their riot at four-thirty
can something be done about the birds

aside from all this I am just fine
and in any case I have to admit
its better than the alternative right

poet and pond with ducks

where did the time go
he slept on a couch
watched the sparrows
he went somewhere
he did something
he made remarkable plans
he forgot the next morning

he was uncomfortable
you could say that

everyone else did everything
carried signs
raised money
spent hours on the phone

so much for that
and now these ducks
consider the grace the confidence

there were six
drifting on a lacquered pond
coined golden in deep green

they have been here
a thousand years
sky lofters
inland comforters

noontime

where god is
evil cannot be absolute

god bless iraq
god bless iran
god bless north korea

god forgive their sins

god bless us who say this
who want to be forgiven

morning of the wedding

I said to the rabbi
you have great suspenders
he had on these two columns
printed with betty boops
he said he liked them
but his wife had reservations

this rabbi once wrestled
around the circuit in europe
he was a professional
that was when he was younger
but he was still burly
you could say if he were not peaceful
he had awkward hands for a brawl

a friend from brooklyn
told me recently
the rabbi did not have suspenders
they were tefillins
the rabbi was wearing

the word is yiddish
you spell it anyway you can
you can do that
if you were brought up in flatbush

but haste to the wedding
I read the contract
and the heavens sighed
boo boop a doop

northern lights

mountain above anchorage

the sleeping lady
says to this sprawling city
be calm don't be profligate
husband your resources
there is the day
and there is the night

anyone who knows how to rest
will not waste time

surprise glacier

beneath this blue sky
a valley blocked with ice
ancient as this cold land
a frozen blue seemingly fired from within
packed hexagonals
fisted of snowflakes
tinged with the glint of a gun barrel
or the soft eyes of lovers

the inlet shudders
when the ice cracks
and a shelf slides into the sound
or shatters into islands of coins
these berkies and growlers
where seals can warm in sunlight
while the otters drift on their backs
and tolerate our good afternoon

down from the mountains

the yearling moose is all body
and four spindly legs
he studies our neighbors shrubs
enjoys their springtime blossoms
nibbles only the best ones

ladies of the klondike

I have been reading about them
several married well of course
and grew old in high society
became founding women
honored as pioneers

trusted too in the old days
they hid stashes for the miners
kept them in safekeeping
better than banks could

others degraded dulled and sickened
took their own shattered lives

there was one had beautiful hair
she washed the feet of the sourdoughs
they had bunions the size of
unbelievable nuggets
moose hides for calluses
she did this

piece of cloth

printed cotton a flower design
green leaves and small
sunbursts in eight petals
a gift from jupik women

let me see about the size
my hand upraised measures the strip
from the nail of my middle finger
down to my thumb the second joint
and the length is three hands or a little less
bound here in a small roll
with red yarn tied off with a bow

mine is one from a basketful
for curious people
the jupik women will never see

something of no value
that I will take home and frame
what they left here for us so priceless

fort richardson memorial day

those honored this day
and those who lost them

the sun in windswept clouds
that wind still winter in shadows
troubling the impassive mourners
who lost these remembered here

there are speeches
presentations of many wreaths

now a circle of trumpets
echoes and re-echoes their farewell calls
three final notes for days end
as we stand in this place
among memories
as deep as these graves

the christmas revels

this christmas eve
it seems held for the season
this faraway place
the distant mountain
brushed with a soft blue haze
and a ruin displaced here
an ancient chapel and tower
habakkuk it may be
keeping his watch here

collage for the year turning
these yellow plums swollen with sunrise
my random recollection
cheering this winter freezing in the mind
how the blossoms came
suddenly a spring wide eyed in surprise
and here is this lovely scripture
the small heart beating under marys heart

the south sky is bright with a half moon
the little town is dusted with frost
the cold steady as a compass needle

and now a chorus reports
a snowfall of angels
caroling the small flickering lights of the town
measuring a shadow
a darkness that says watch in peace
and I look for a sign

the one that I did not hear you promise
when the lights went out

well now a christmas card
the first of the season
what does it say

it says his mother gave him
a rattle her small dark child
and he shook the world

then on that starstruck night
after the snowfall of angels
everyone heard the heavens singing
and even the ox and ass
perked up their ears and bawled
they did not know which way to turn
and we could do no better

then the shepherds came dancing in
came dancing from the hills
all the way to the stable
and we could shut our doors then
seal them against the cold
with yesterdays papers
and kindle ourselves new fires

now in the decades since
people have been cheering their windows

with candles and glass lights
and saying welcome on their doors
with holly wreaths and ribbons

I want to shake your hand
it has been like this every year since

the wise men came later
it is not easy to say when
not on that first night surely
but herod was still living
that master of murdering

these patient old men
they had waited so long for the right sign
these men of the world the wise ones

and when they came to that home
they fell on their knees
before the radiant child
oh how often does it happen
the quest of a lifetime fulfilled

their gifts are well known today
the gold the frankincense the myrrh
and these men understood
how costly the offerings were
how they had traded their youth for palsied hands
and why it was worth it they had come so far

they never returned to herod
well no of course not

not to the murdering old fox
there was the matter of the dream
their dream celeste
reserved only for the ardent
that dream from the angels told them
avoid the capital if you can
take your journey home through new orleans
enjoy the shrove tide festival
now the waters have receded
the crepe suzettes are delicious

and this is all we know
and this is more than enough
as the great dreams of our lives are

when christ came to town
he skated on our pond
the snowballs we packed with stones
melted in our hands

our lady our mother
once you carried
and protected
the child jesus
please walk with us now
when he calls us home

epilogue

lines for a new beginning

I know where I will go to make my choice
for this country's new executive
and I pray the man will do right by his oath

I probably will not live to see the day
that he will conclude his term of office
but I wish him all the best

I wish him years of fruitful service
for all of us and our troubled world
and a serene evening when that service is done

we have yet as a people
so many gifts to offer this small planet
may he bring to this world a great heart
and a generosity in our name

and pray God that this country becomes
under his steady hands
the best that it was founded to be

walking in snow

shutting down
time to walk in the snow

make footprints where there are none
only the crooked marks of the dogs

mooch or joe the best of dogs

it is good coming down this slope

the dogs have been buried
how long now

oh these many years

today the leafless trees
gleam in the morning sun
with crowns of beaten gold

it is not surprising
the prints should appear this morning
old mooch and faithful joe

you have my meaning
where there is no coherence
just what is good to remember
or to forget

it is like this
you go alone in the morning
your thoughts running on and on
until they come wagging home

Other books by Pearn and Associates, Inc.

I Look Around for my Life, John Knoepfle

Ikaria, Anita Sullivan

The U Book, Nathan Preston Pierce

Another Chance, Joe Naiman

Goulash and Picking Pickles, Louise Hoffmann

Point Guard, Victor Pearn

www.ingramcontent.com/pod-product-compliance
Lightning Source LLC
Chambersburg PA
CBHW031321150426
43191CB00005B/283